# France

## Children's travel activity book and journal

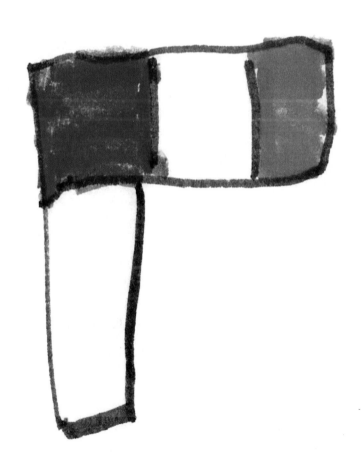

tinytourists

explore. discover. learn.

Hello!

My name's Topher*
and I love adventures!

I'll be keeping you company on your journey through this book. Look out for me, I'll be popping up every now and again.

Count how many times you can spot me...I'm quite good at hiding...

**\*Topher** is named after St. Chris**topher**, the patron saint for travellers who is known for keeping all those who travel safe from harm. Check out his story on our website plus free activity sheets on keeping safe on holiday and how to be a responsible tiny tourist: www.tinytourists.co.uk

**tinytourists** is all about inspiring family travel and making the most of adventures; keeping travel meaningful and memorable, educational and fun. Visit us on Facebook to find out more and to join the tinytourists' community.

Written and Designed by Louise Amodio
Illustrated by Louise Amodio and Catherine Mantle
Cover Illustration by Giacomo (age 7)

Published by Beans and Joy Publishing Ltd as a product from Tiny Tourists Ltd, Great Britain.
www.beansandjoy.com

ISBN:978-1-912293-58-2

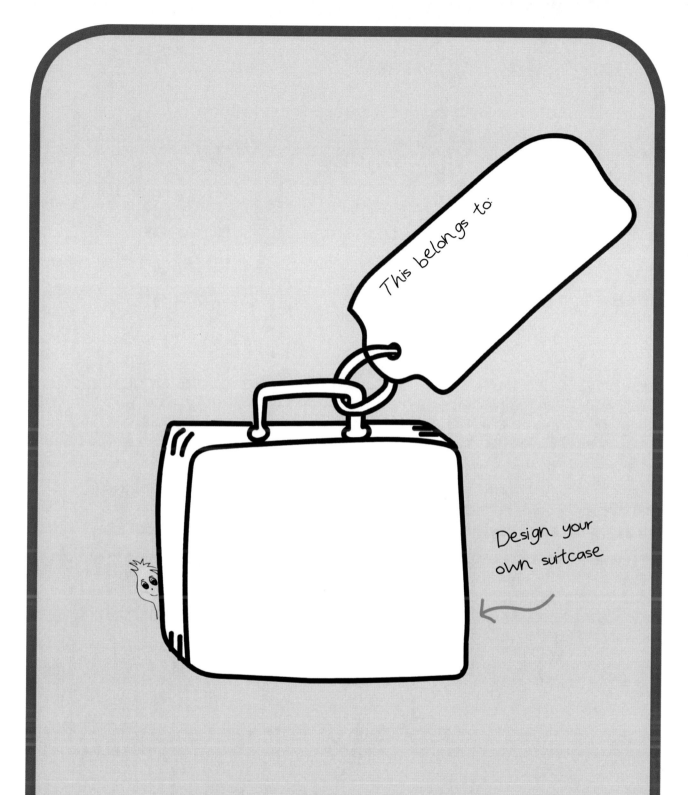

This belongs to:

Design your own suitcase

Your adventure starts here

# How to use this book

Welcome to your fabulously fun-packed French activity book!

Look out for these symbols to tell you what type of activity you'll be doing:

 for writing and recording and solving puzzles

 for drawing and colouring and being creative

## Time to get started!

### Section 1: My Travel Log

Show off your planning skills; when you are going, where you are going, who you're going with, what the weather will be like, and what you'll pack in your suitcase. This will help form part of a lovely keepsake as well as get you organised!

### Section 2: Epic Explorer Skills

Time for some fun - full of games and activities for a bit of France-themed fun, as well as practice your extraordinary explorer skills;

**PROBLEM-SOLVING (MATHS), CODE-BREAKING AND COMMUNICATING (LITERACY AND LANGUAGES) AND SPY SKILLS (SCIENCE AND GEOGRAPHY). SEE INDEX FOR INFO.**

Want to learn some French words too? Look out for some new words you can practice while you're on your trip. We give you the real French spelling and how they sound too. Have a practice with these three important words:

phrase: bonjour
say: (bon-jaw)
meaning: hello

phrase: merci
say: (mur-see)
meaning: thank you

phrase: s'il vous plait
say: (seel vu play)
meaning: please

### Section 3: Memory Bank

This is where you can record all the memories from your trip. The perfect finishing touch to a lovely book of holiday memories; what you did, what you ate, what you saw, what you collected, and fun lists for recording the best bits and the worst bits.

## Bon Voyage!

# My Info

Me:

My home address:

Eye Colour:

Hair Colour:

Distinguishing features:

How long is your right index finger?

0  1  2  3  4  5  6  7  8  9  10  11  12  13  14  15  16 cm

My Destination:

Arrival:

Date: _____

Passport Stamp:

Departure:

Date: _____

# Where am I going?

Mark with an **X** where you're going to in France:

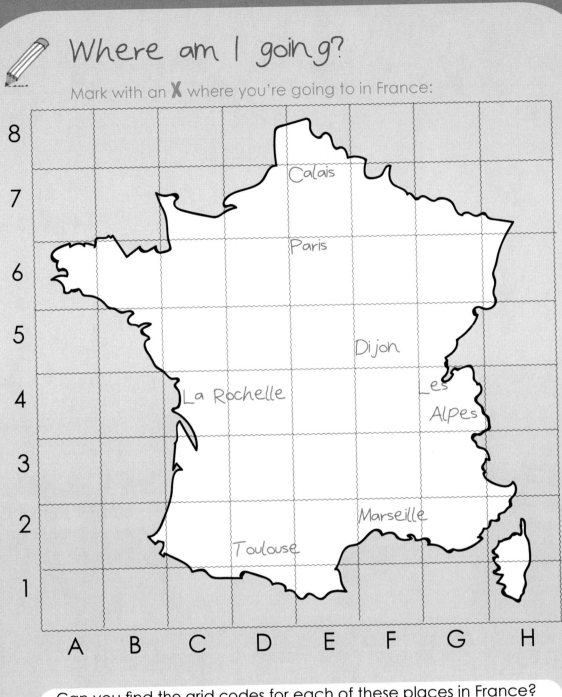

Can you find the grid codes for each of these places in France?

Paris: E6          Dijon:          Marseille          Calais:

Where are you staying?

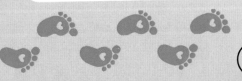

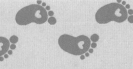

6

# How will I get there?

How will you get to France and how many hours on each type of transport will you spend? Add it all up for the grand total:

| | Hours Travelled |
|---|---|
| Un avion (un av-ee-on) | |
| Un bus (un bus) | |
| Une voiture (oon vwa-chur) | |
| Un train (un tran) | |
| Un bateau (un bat-oh) | |
| Grand Total: | |

# What am I taking with me?

Can you write or draw 6 things you will pack in your bag?

# Who am I going with?

Draw a picture of who you're going on holiday with in the frame below:

Can you learn their names in french?

Example

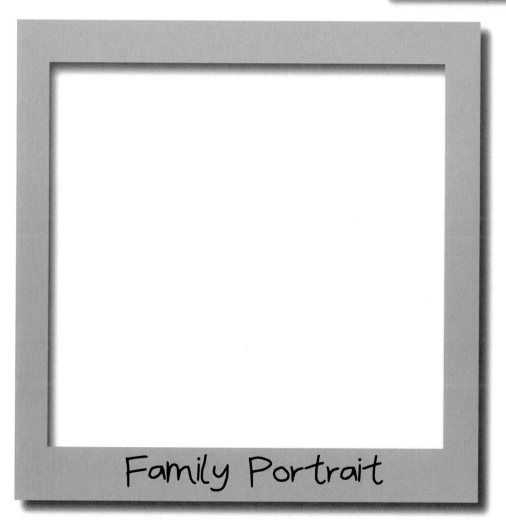

Family Portrait

| Ma maman | Mon papa | Mon frere | Ma soeur | Mes grand-parents |
|----------|----------|-----------|----------|-------------------|
| (ma mamon) | (mon papa) | (mon frair) | (ma sur) | (mes grond-paronts) |
| My mummy | My daddy | My brother | My sister | My grandparents |

# What will the weather be like?

Draw a circle around the weather you predict you'll have, and then record the actual weather you really do have:

Il pleut
*(eel pl)*
It's raining

Il fait beau
*(eel fay bow)*
It's sunny

Il neige
*(eel nej)*
It's snowing

What weather DID you have?
Was your prediction correct?

# Epic Explorer Skills

**PROBLEM-SOLVING (MATHS)**

**CODE-BREAKING & COMMS (LITERACY & LANGUAGES)**

**SPY SKILLS (SCIENCE, GEOGRAPHY)**

# Il Tricolore

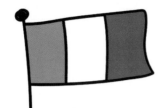

This is the French flag, with 3 colours, blue, white and red.

**How many flags can you spot on your travels?**

*Colour in this flag*

| bleu | blanc | rouge |
|------|-------|-------|
| *(ble)* | *(blonk)* | *(rooj)* |
| blue | white | red |

12

# Chateux, Escargot, Monet

Can you find these famous French items in the wordsearch?

## Wordsearch

```
C M E R V U O L E L
L R O G R A P E S E
P O O N D S M O S S
O L P I E R W C O A
G R A P S T A P L L
S B A R I S R U C P
C R X A E T A H C E
G I M E O L G N N S
L E S C A R G O T C
```

 ESCARGOT

 CHATEAU

 LE LOUVRE

 CRIOSSANT

 MONET

 LES ALPES

 GRAPES

 BRIE

# Cycling

Cycling is one of the most popular sports in France.
See how many bikes you can spot while you're there.
Help the cycling captain choose his team for the next big
race. He only wants to choose cyclists with shirt numbers in the
3 times table:

Find all the 3s

# Football 5s

The Paris football manager wants to pick a team using players with shirts that are in the 5 times table. Can you circle all the shirts below that he would need to choose?

Find all the 5s

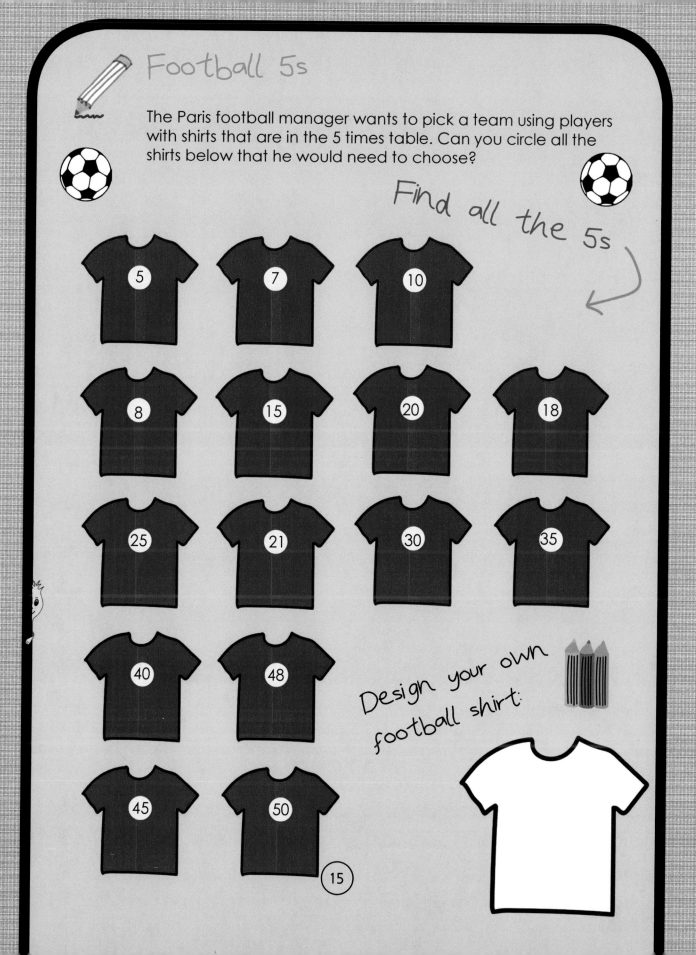

5  7  10

8  15  20  18

25  21  30  35

40  48

Design your own football shirt:

45  50

15

# Boulangerie

A bakery in France is called un boulangerie (boo-lonj-ery) The owner of the boulangerie below has a large order today and needs 10 of each type of bread and pastry.

Looking at what he already has on his shelves, can you work out how many extra he needs to make to equal 10?

# To make 10, how many more are needed??

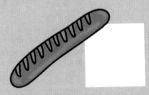

il baguette
(eel bag ett)
long bread stick

un croissant
(un cruh-sont)
crescent shaped pastry

du pain
(doo pan)
loaf of bread

un pain au raisin
(un pan oh raisin)
raisin pastry

# How long is your baguette?!

Use the chart below to measure how many cm long each of the baguettes are. Which is the longest?

Measure up

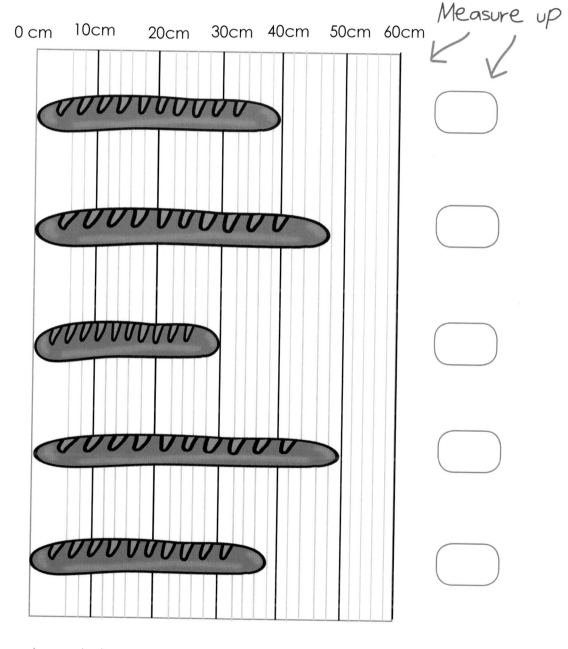

| un | deux | trois | quattre | cinq | six | sette | huit | neuf | dix |
|----|------|-------|---------|------|-----|-------|------|------|-----|
| *un* | *der* | *twa* | *cat* | *sank* | *sees* | *set* | *weet* | *nerf* | *dees* |
| 1 | 2 | 3 | 4 | 5 | 6 | 7 | 8 | 9 | 10 |

 Fromage!

Rue Montorgueil is a bustling area in the heart of Paris. Its street markets and shops sell some of the best meat, fish and cheese in the city.

A french cheese shop is called a fromagerie (from-arj-ari).
This fromagerie needs to make more cheese so it has 20 of each.
Can you help?

Add some to make 20

 + ☐ = 20

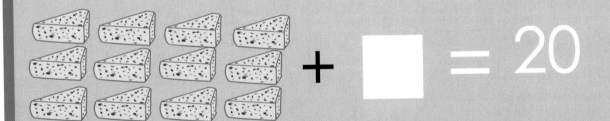 + ☐ = 20

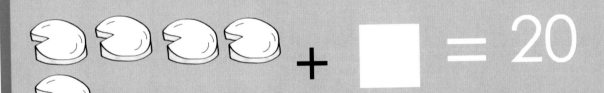 + ☐ = 20

 + ☐ = 20

# Cheeses for €20

In each row of cheeses below, every row must add up to €20.
Can you complete the blank labels with the missing prices?

Fill in the blanks

€5 + €10 + ___ = 20

€8 + €3 + ___ = 20

€8 + €8 + ___ = 20

€12 + €5 + ___ = 20

19

# Vin

France is famous for growing juicy grapes and turning them into tasty wine!

Follow the journey of this bunch of grapes through the maze...

The first stage of wine-making is the crushing of the grapes to release the juice and let it mix with the grape skin flavours and colours.

Some wine-makers do this squishing with their feet!

Follow the grapes

# Fromage Sudoku

There are over 300 different types of cheese in France. A different one for each day of the year. Can you draw cheese? Complete the gaps below, following the sudoku rules...

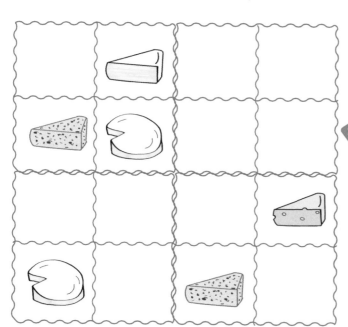

### Fill in the gaps

Each item must appear ONCE in every row and every column, so think carefully...

What's your favourite french cheese?

# Escargot

Some people in France enjoy eating cooked snails! They are called Escargot (escargo) and are often cooked in butter and a herb called parsley. Would you like to try one?

Colour me in

# Cote d'Azur - Yacht Spotting

In the south of France by the sea is The Cote d'Azur - a collection of beautiful sea-side towns along the beach where people like to live, holiday, and moor up in their very posh boats. If you visit this area, you will see lots and lots of boats!

Spot the 5 differences between these two boats:

## Spot the

## difference

# Shopping in Sunny St Tropez

St Tropez is a sunny town in the Cote D'Azur and you might spot lots of pretty shops selling designer shoes, handbags and clothes. Look out for the best dressed person!

Check out the ladies below, read the descriptions, and work out...

## ...Who is who?

### Michelle
1. Loves blue
2. Has brown hair
3. Likes to wear the same colour shoes as her handbag

### Camille
1. Has short hair
2. Has the same colour handbag as Adrienne
3. Didn't do much shopping today

### Adrienne
1. Has the same colour dress as Camille's shoes
2. Has long hair
3. Has black shoes

# Le Tour De Eiffel

The Eiffel Tower is France's most famous monument. It was built in 1889 to celebrate the 100 year anniversary of the French Revolution. You can catch a lift to the top, or climb the 1,700 steps to the middle platform.

Colour in the tower

Copy the tower onto here

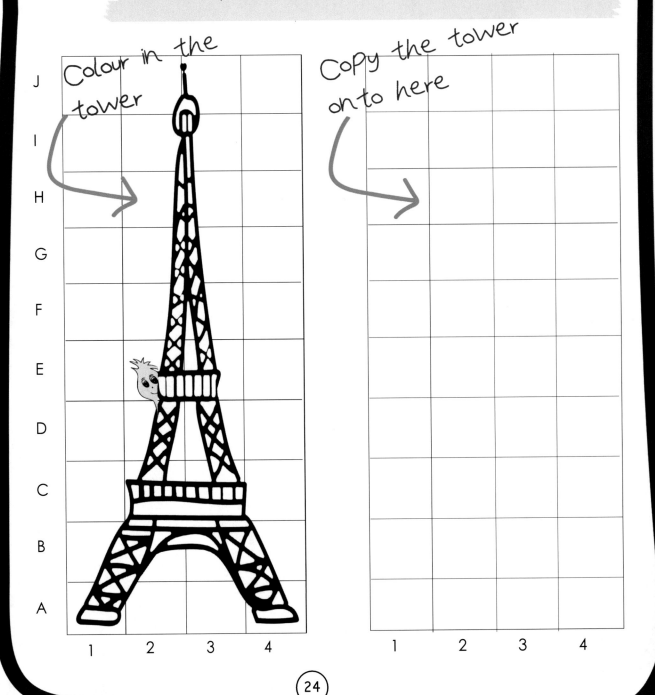

24

# Arc de Triomphe

The Arc de Triomphe (*ark dee tree-omf*) was ordered to be built by the Emporer Napoleon in 1806 to honour and celebrate the brave french soldiers that had fought and won many battles during the French Revolution and in the following battles across Europe.

Every night, a candle is lit at the bottom to remember all the soldiers that died during battle.

Colour me in

# Parlais Francais !

Learning a few french words to use during your travels will help you to be polite, and also handy when making new friends!

See how many of these phrases you can try out...

## Bonjour!

*Bon-jaw*
Hello

## Merci Beaucoup!

*Mer-si Bow-coop*
Thank you very much

## S'il vous Plait

*Seal vu play*
Please

## Comment t'appelles tu?

*Common tapell too*
What is your name?

## C'est bon
*Se bon*
It's good

## C'est combien?
*Se combee-an*
How much is it?

## Je m'appelle <name>
*Ju Mapelle <name>*
My name is <name>

## Ou est le <place>
*Oo eh le <place>*
Where is the <place>

## Au revoir
*Or rev-wah*
Goodbye

# Mont Blanc and Skiing

Mont Blanc is the highest mountain in France, and the highest in all of Europe. It is 4,808metres tall and is snowy and icy on the top.
People ski down the mountains around Mont Blanc in both France and Italy, every winter. Have you ever been?
Look carefully at the skiers below.
One is a tiny bit different to the others............can you spot him?

spot the odd one out

# Fondue

After a morning skiing, you will be hungry! You might find a hot fondue will warm you up. You can dip all sorts of things into the cheesy fondue sauce. Some of the most popuar ingredients are below.

Match the french word to the picture

Pomme     Pain      Boeuf      Fromage

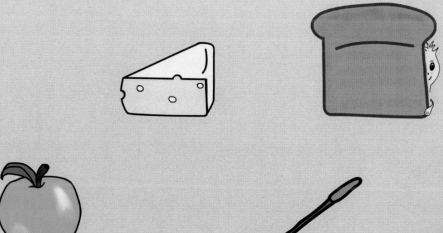

# Metro Journeys

In Paris, there is an underground train network called Le Metro. The first Metro line was opened in 1900 - it's very old!

Start at the Metro station below and follow the directions to see which famous landmark you end up at:

Go East 3 Places. Go North 5 Places. Go East 2 Places. Circle the landmark you arrive at!

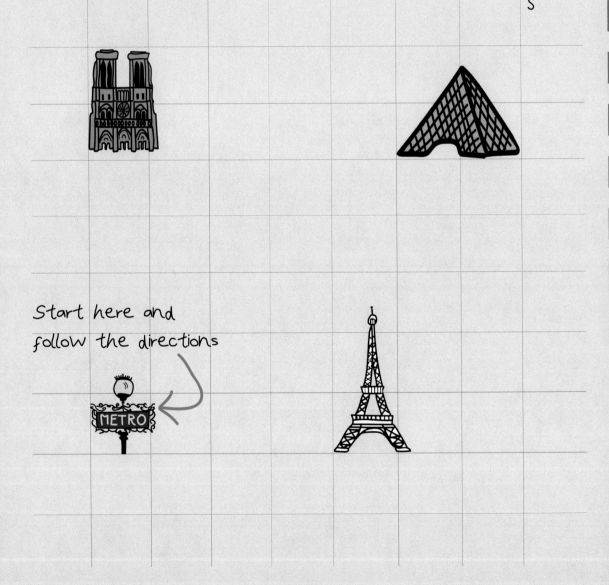

Start here and follow the directions

METRO

# A Curious Smile

Le Louvre is a famous art gallery in Paris with an entrance marked by a glass pyramid. Inside is one of the world's most famous paintings, The Mona Lisa. The lady in the painting is famous for her smile. Can you draw a smile on the lady below, and fill in the rest of the frames with artwork of your own?

Fill the frames with your own artwork...

# A Bridge, A Pond, and Waterlillies

One of France's most famous artists was Claude Monet, an artist who loved to draw gardens, flowers, seaside paintings and sunrises and sunsets. This painting is one of his most famous "A Bridge over a Pond of Waterlillies".....................................................can you draw it too?

Copy or draw your own
waterlillies picture

# Grapes

French vinyards grow many grape varieties and use them to make some of the world's best wines and champagnes.

Champagne is made from only three types of grape: Chardonnay (a white grape), Pinot Noir (a red grape) and Pinot Meunier (a red grape). The makers use careful quantities of each grape juice to get the perfect flavour. They never let the skin get mixed in otherwise it would turn the champagne a red colour!

*Colour in the blank bunches using the pattern* ⟩

Do you like grapes?

# Chateaux

France no longer has a royal family but it does still have many beautiful palaces, called chateaux (shat-oh), all around the country that can be visited, stayed at, or bought to live in.

Two of the most famous chateaux are called Versailles and Chambord.

Colour the chateau

# France Quiz

How much do you think you know about France?

Answer these questions to find out... the answers can be found in this book! Good luck! Bon Chance!

In which town would you find this famous tower?

_____

Can you name 3 french cheeses?

_____

_____

What fruit is wine made from?

_____

Which type of french shop sells bread?

_____

What's the name of the famous painting in Paris of a lady with a curious smile?

_____

What is the tallest mountain in France called?

_____

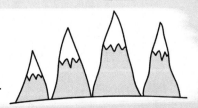

# Memory Bank

It's time to write down all the things you've
done, seen and tasted on your trip!

**WRITE, DRAW, STAPLE, STICK**

# A Place to Stay

Where are you staying in France? Is it a hotel?
A house? A chalet? An apartment? Something else?

Can you **draw a picture** of it here?

# Home Sweet Home

Can you **draw a picture** of where you live back at home?

What is different about this and your holiday home?

39

# What have you eaten?

**Draw some food** you have eaten on holiday on the plate below.
What was your favourite?

# What adventures have you had?

**Write a postcard** about your adventures, and design a nice stamp:

Carte Postale

(41)

# Momento Board

Stick bits and pieces on these pages that you've collected during your trip; favourite tickets, receipts, leaflets, drawings...

# Daily Diary

Note down some of the different things you have done each day:

Monday

Tuesday

Wednesday

Thursday

Friday

Saturday

Sunday

# Memory Gallery

Draw pictures or doodles of any special memories:

# The Good and The Bad

Time to think about the best bits and the worst bits:

The best three things →

The Worst three things

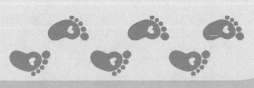

# Chitter Chatter

Talk with your family about these questions to help fill in the gaps:

Something I did for the first time:

Something I want to tell everyone when I get home:

Something that made me laugh:

Something I did that was brave:

Something I want to do again:

# Index

(what's in this book and where you can find it)

# Au Revoir

(goodbye, until next time)

I hope you enjoyed your adventure and completing this book along the way.

How many times did you spot me?

_____

Keep safe!
Love from
Topher xx

# Where would you like to go next?

Spain

USA

Greece

Italy

Egypt

China

UK

Australia

South Africa

Thailand

Mexico

Finland

Made in the USA
Middletown, DE
17 December 2022

19344800R00029